ENTREPREN

The Life of an Entrepreneur in 90 Pages

"There's an Amazing Story Behind Every Story"

Patrick Bet-David

With

Thomas N. Ellsworth

Published in the United States by Valuetainment Publishing

Quotes by current or historical public figures and the descriptions of their lives and acts were taken from public sources assumed to be credible and were researched and vetted as much as possible. The authors do not make any absolute claim as to their accuracy.

ISBN: 978-0-9974410-0-0

DEDICATION

For Tico, Dylan, Senna, Bailey and Brooke -
We love you!

CONTENTS

ACKNOWLEDGMENTS

No book is complete without offering thanks to those who inspired its development.

First, hugs and kisses to our respective wives who remind us every day just how lucky we are to be married to anyone at all, let alone them!

Second, to our dedicated editor Rebecca Livermore. From smart quotes to run on sentences, she is a real pro and added polish to the final manuscript.

Third, we bow to the entrepreneurs who went before us and have inspired, educated and encouraged us up to this point in our journey. The list is long and distinguished.

Fourth, we applaud the entrepreneurs that we have had the privilege of cheering for as they found their vision and went after it with the dedication of an "all timer."

Last, but not least, we thank the aspiring entrepreneurs everywhere who have visited Valuetainment.com, read any of our previous books, or worked with us at startups including the PHP Agency Inc. Let us all remember the quote of Sir Winston Churchill:

"NEVER, NEVER, NEVER GIVE UP"

INTRODUCTION

Viral videos are like tornadoes. They are not planned as much as they simply happen with colossal and exciting effect when the conditions are right.

In mid-October 2015 I wanted to communicate a message about entrepreneurs and decided to create a short video titled "The Life of an Entrepreneur in 90 Seconds" You can see that video at this link:

www.patrickbetdavid.com/life-entrepreneur-90-seconds/

The original intent was to share a compelling and emotional glimpse into the story behind the average entrepreneur. Many people see the end product and have no idea what it takes to get there. These people have not been exposed to the process. Like making sausage, there's a part of life that some people probably don't want to see because it's messy.

Roughly an hour after posting on Facebook, it had gone over 50,000 views, and I was obviously pleased. Overnight things got weird. The next morning, I noticed it had crossed over 2,000,000 views, and just hours later it was deep into the millions, and I knew it was viral. By the end of the weekend it had hit 15,000,000 views and was still growing. Today, in mid-2016, it has amassed over 27,000,000 views and it is still viewed thousands of times each day.

Why did such a simple video receive such an overwhelming response?

There are many reasons – but the best answer seems to be that the video captured the simple truth and wrapped it in an emotional story in which everyone can relate . We all know failure. We all understand challenges. We all have experienced some little victories in life here-n-there even if our life has had its share of tragedies and isn't much to talk about at the moment. Everyone seemed to 'get' the video in some way from some angle even if it was an aspirational yearning covered in tears from deep inside that merely cried out, "Someday…"

Along the way, thousands of people (maybe you) asked if the story and concepts in the video could be captured in a book that people could use to build their own personal plan. I thought that was a good idea - so I did.

If you watched the video carefully, then you will recognize the subtle themes that I have expanded into chapters. In these pages, I DON'T tell you what business to pursue as an entrepreneur or where is the best place to live, but I DO present a framework that explains how to build your own plan and what to do to stay on track. As for why you take the plunge – that's deeply personal, but I absolutely assume that you have a burning desire deep in your heart. All said, here is the outline of the chapters:

1. The Truth – Accepting Reality
2. Vision – Looking Forward
3. Commitment – Staying with Your Vision
4. Resiliency – Recovering from Setbacks
5. Validation – Experiencing Confirmation
6. Drifting or Driving – A Challenge to You

HOW TO USE THIS BOOK

This book will not take you very long to read and that's *exactly* the point.

The purpose of this book is for you to understand the six points on the path to the life of an entrepreneur and embrace the challenge to drive forward every day. This book sets the table for you to envision what your future will be.

As this book prepares to be published, my wife and I just had a new baby girl, Senna.. She joins her two brothers in a very full (and noisy) household.

This entire parenting experience made me think about how funny life can be at times. Not so long ago I was the 28 year-old entrepreneur who was competing at the highest level in my trade and was so focused that there was no desire to get married or do much of anything else for that matter. My level of focus was intense. Those who worked with me at that time often call it other words and I don't need to give you the list. I knew that I had a special intensity but didn't want anything or anyone to distract me or slow me down from my long-term vision.

I thought getting married and building a family was

going to slow me down. On a side note, I love kids. If I had it my way, I would have 20 kids. I literally mean that. Close your eyes and listen closely – that's my wife screaming after I said "20 kids."

What's strange is that the intensity has actually increased since having kids. The clarity of purpose and the desire to win is at an all-time high. Wisdom and experience definitely helps in knowing how to process certain issues I may have not known eight years ago but regardless I would do anything to win for these kids.

You may be asking what's my purpose of this little rant and why is it here prior to chapter one. Well, the reality of it is that today I have the honor to mentor many entrepreneurs around the world directly or indirectly and one of the things that always comes up is how to consistently stay focused and maintain the excitement you had in the beginning.

To me it comes down to why you do what you do? What makes you tick? What moves you? What can get you to tears within seconds? What thought can you think about and within 30 seconds you could absolutely get emotional or absolutely frustrated?

Why don't you tap into that more often? Why don't

you have private conversations with yourself on why you're not giving it your best?

I think that too often people merely read quotes or motivational messages about dreams.

"Chase your dreams!"

"Never give up on your dreams."

"Take hold of your best life now!"

I'm guilty of it as well. Not because it is a good or a bad thing but because it's a healthy thing to do.

The opposite of a dream is a nightmare. How often do you think about THE nightmare? I'm not talking about Freddy Krueger from the famous Nightmare on Elm Street horror movie, but the nightmare of a life lived in which you:

Did NOTHING.

You didn't change.

Your chose to live a small life.

Can you imagine what that life is going to look like in five, 10 or even 20 years? That's the nightmare I am talking about. It's one horrifying thought after another coming after you just like Freddy Krueger:

What's your personal life going to look like?

How is your marriage going to be doing?

How will you be doing with your kids?

Will you even still be married?

How will you be doing financially?

Will you be able to help your aging parents out if help is needed?

Will you be OK being the person where you wasted your life never really giving your best to one thing?

Instead will you become a fan of LeBron James, Ronaldo, Messi or someone else?

Will you be able to look at your kids in the face knowing you gave everything you had to win for them?

Will your kids secretly be asking themselves why did my Daddy or Mommy give up?

Or imagine the one time they get upset with you and they actually tell you that in your face while you're 53 years old or even worse 70 years old?

They'll probably come back and apologize because they know they hurt you but were they correct? You'll be asking yourself that forever. When you face yourself in the mirror following their comments, how will you look at yourself?

These are the thoughts I have when I think about why I do what I do. I look at a few pictures and it taps into a certain emotion I can't describe.

The first one is an epic picture with the sun in the background and my oldest son in my arms. It is the first time I took him to church. Then there's the one of his first time seeing snow. It's in Big Bear in the mountains outside Los Angeles. I keep it with a picture of the first time I brought him to my office at a time where our startup business was on the verge of either making it or failing like so many others.

I share these pictures with you because I want you to form mental pictures of special times. I feel sometimes we forget what we're really fighting for. We forget why we're entrepreneurs. We forget why we do what we do. We forget why we work late hours. We forget the bigger picture.

It's the mental struggle of thinking we have to be there all the time to be the best father versus the example we teach for them to learn how to survive on their own when they're adults. How many kids grow up in an environment where their father comes home at 5:30pm working a 9 to 5, thinking they have to do the same? And we wonder why the financial struggle continues generationally.

I want my kids to know the power of entrepreneurship. I want them to be future leaders of the world in anything they choose to do. I want them to choose to be leaders when they see their dad enjoying his craft with all his heart.

As you start chapter one, my simple message to you is, take an hour or two away on a Sunday and get away from everyone. Talk to yourself and ask yourself tough questions. Be direct. Don't hold back. Envision two versions of yourself talking to you. One the leader who steps out and takes a chance and the other is the one who's been holding you back and makes excuses.

Make this private two way conversation your opportunity to remind yourself of why you are choosing to become an entrepreneur. Don't feel sorry for yourself on the hours you put in, instead be proud of the example you're setting to win for those who are counting on you.

And for those of you very young entrepreneurs who say "what do I do if I don't have any kids," my reason was my Father for many years. I could sit there and think about him for 30 seconds and get so emotional and jacked up that I could run through a wall at full speed.

Find your reason! Find what gets you to tick! Find what gets you frustrated! And put it in front of your face over and over again until you are determined to WIN for that reason. For some of you it may be YOU winning for YOU to validate the fact that you're the winner you always thought you were.

Regardless of what it is, make sure it's something that at any point if you tap into, it'll bring you to tears. This is your personal motivational tool. And unlike a cheap weekend seminar… it's 100% real.

Are you ready to begin? Then let's start your personal journey to discover the principles that will show you how to forge your path.

Good luck!

1

THE TRUTH

The reality behind what you see

"The truth will set you free, but first it will piss you off."

– Gloria Steinem

The moment you accept or admit the truth in a tough life situation is the moment you feel relief. That relief may also carry consequences but it is relief nonetheless.

You may *admit* to having done something wrong and feel relief because you are no longer hiding and carrying fear or anxiety. This may include going to jail! I've seen criminals interviewed and say "I felt relief" when asked what it felt like when they were caught.

You may *accept* the truth of a situation and made an important decision to go do something you knew you had to do but ignoring the truth was holding you back. I've talked to many friends who broke off bad relationships or quit dead-end jobs long after they knew the truth of the situation.

The interesting part of this is the truth is usually incredibly simple. It boils down to a spark in your life that lights the fire that leads to action. That spark may be you looking in the mirror one day and finally being honest about what you see -or- listening to a friend who urges you to be honest with yourself. Either spark typically leads to a simple admission: "Yes, I lied" or "I'm kidding myself, this isn't working."

The good news is this: from that point on, the reality of what you see is grounded in objectivity – you see the truth of the situation.

"Most people only pay attention to the final product of a successful entrepreneur. They say things like, "I can never be like them" or "They got lucky." What most don't see is what they've overcome. All the struggles, the daily rejections, the heartaches, the betrayals, the rumors, the criticism, the empty bank account, and all those lonely nights while trying to make their vision a reality.

You see the only difference between the one who quits and the one who doesn't is that they showed up every day. They worked hard every day. They hustled every day. They learned from a proven mentor every day. They improve every day. They did all this even though they felt like quitting every day. And eventually they became who they are today."

You just read the narration from the video "The Life of an Entrepreneur in 90 seconds." It's the one referenced in the introduction of this book, and as you read this, it has been viewed over 27 million times. The dialogue is clear, concise and simple. How did such a simple message resonate so deeply, so suddenly, and so broadly with so many people?

I believe that simple truths hit the mind and heart the hardest – and therein lies their power. The dialogue was simple and crisp while the visuals were compelling and relatable to the average individual. Relatable to who they dream to be tomorrow and who they confess to be today. That is, if they trust someone else enough to face the truth and boldly make that confession.

When you talk to people and ask why they are who they are today, the answer you get is a long explanation almost always describing what happened to them in life up to this point. They see their explanations as reasons. In reality, these are excuses. Controllable or uncontrollable, they are excuses just the same. You will invariably hear about parents, school, bad neighborhoods, the wrong friends, divorces and other situations that certainly impacted their lives. Yes, some of the unfortunate life havoc was beyond their control in childhood when they were helpless passengers on the speeding train of life. It happens.

If you listen closely, you will rarely hear any ownership of even the smallest part of the narrative or, worse still, ownership about what they are doing about it today. It they are doing nothing, don't they need to own that truth?

It's easy to play the part of the victim and make explanations about what happened to you because it gives you a reason (which I will always call an excuse) NOT to do anything except talk about how you got here and how life treated you so badly along the way. Now, it's not necessarily bad to talk about how you got here – that can be your story. But it's just plain tragic to allow it to become the excuse that allows you to stay here.

Your story can be a powerful motivating force if, and only if you allow it to be. Otherwise, it's a long explanation which ends up being an excuse.

A story is honest and compelling and explains what moves you and drives you forward. For example, I grew up in Iran; the leader was deposed, and civil unrest broke out everywhere. It was horrible. My father boldly escaped and took our family to a refugee camp in Germany where we waited for our opportunity to come to the USA. We settled in Southern California, and you cannot possibly underestimate how happy we were to get there. After high school I joined the Army and served in the 101st Airborne. After that, I got into financial services. That's my story.

Did you read that because I did not go to private school in Los Angeles, I didn't go to an Ivy League college? Or, if only I wasn't an immigrant I would have more opportunities? No, you didn't – those would be excuses. Do you see the difference?

Here's a tip, every time you hear if only or because, ask the person to stop and ask them, "Where are you in this?" They will probably stammer and ask what you mean. Then say, "We all have a story, and life can be tough. But the truth is we are not tied to yesterday. Have you taken 100% ownership for what you do about it today?" I predict you will hear "But you don't understand…" or "Let me explain how terrible it was and what it did to me…" The best thing you can say to them or YOURSELF, if you are the one saying those things to yourself, is this: "The truth about the past is, yes, your life had issues yesterday, and some of them were not your fault. The truth about today is you have a responsibility to do something about it versus use yesterday as an excuse to do nothing today and have no plan when you wake up tomorrow."

After reading this book, if you do nothing more than accept the truth of who and why you are who you are today, AND accept the corresponding truth that you have a responsibility to make a plan to change that situation, then I have already left you better than I found you. Entrepreneurs escape from the lie of ongoing victimhood by accepting the truth that they are responsible to effect change in their life. They work or invent their way out and do so without hesitation or excuse. Entrepreneurs have a story.

If you have ever gone on a whitewater rafting trip, then you know that before you float down the river, a good trip guide typically gives an extended talk about the raft, the river, and the risks. It is somewhat startling to hear the guide explain, "In the event that you fall out of the raft, you are the one and only member of your survival party." Huh? No one is going to jump in and help me? Nope, they will first secure the raft and those IN the raft and ONLY THEN come get you. You are responsible to actively save yourself. It doesn't matter whether you made a mistake and fell out or if rough water or someone else's mistake caused you to be thrown out. Either way, you are in the water and the water doesn't care about you. There are no unemployment checks or food stamps to save you, and you can't call 911. The river doesn't stop so someone can come get you. It keeps moving, and you move with it.

The tour guide goes on to explain that YOU are accountable to keep yourself from drowning until you are rescued. You are usually advised to keep your head up, and hold your feet up so you don't get a foot caught in the rocks and branches under the water. You may be reminded to use the paddle, (the one you were supposed to hold on to NO MATTER WHAT) to maneuver yourself until the raft can get in position so you can climb back in. No one argues with the logic presented by the tour guide. No one argues with the truth of how the rushing water will flow. Everyone nods with scrunched eyebrows and panic on their faces.

With that reference in mind, isn't it absolutely shocking that people can accept the truth spoken by a whitewater rafting tour guide but refuse to take any accountability when their life or career "falls out of the raft?" They expect to be saved or seek comfort from others who pat them on the head and agree that life screwed them. Worse, they use how they got to where they are today as an excuse for staying where they are. These people are drowning in the water of life and are making no effort to get back to the raft. They deny the truth altogether or simply refuse to process and accept it. Because, if only, because, if only… Pathetic.

The first step is to accept the truth and commit to move forward regardless of how bad your current situation may be. The funny thing about the raw truth behind why and where you are in life is that it's so difficult to admit when confronted but so easy to own up to when you are alone. It's easy to come clean when there's little risk of being accountable to someone else. We've all heard a friend say to us "Hey, the truth hurts." The pain in the truth is not the truth itself; it comes from the realization that I must accept responsibility for what I do about it – and be accountable to motivate myself to take action.

Sadly, instead of being motivated, many people avoid the pain of the truth (or avoid being pissed off by reality), which can be used as an incredible motivator.

Too many people proceed to focus on the current point in time and launch into waves of because excuses and if only denial about why our life is where it is at that point in time. When they look at others and be envious or jealous, they also tend to only look at the current point in time and make wrong-headed assumptions or cast unfair judgments.

Whether they are in denial about themselves or reaching wrong conclusions about others, the truth of the final product of what they see can be easily misunderstood. They must strive to be receptive to the truth in themselves and others.

Only when you fully accept the truth can the real work begin. There is the story of the doctor who was explaining the devastating truth to a patient, "Listen, Joe, I have some bad news. Looking at your chest X-Ray, it's clear you have lung cancer. I need to start chemotherapy immediately, and your share of the cost is $3,000. Insurance should cover the rest." Joe replied, "Seriously? I have a hard time accepting that I have lung cancer! Furthermore, $3,000 to start treatment seems expensive and crazy." The doctor calmly replied, "Joe, I know the truth is hard to accept. I'll tell you what, for $10 I'll touch-up your X-Rays and you can just go home."

Yes, that's a ridiculous story. But the point is clear: It's never a bad time to face the truth. Let's get real.

Post-It #1

(Stick it where you will see it every day):

1. TRUTH:

I accept the truth of

today's reality

And personally commit

To change it.

2

VISION

Where are you going?

"I got the eye of the tiger,
a fighter, dancing through the fire
'Cause I am a champion
and you're gonna hear me roar"
– Katy Perry, Roar

Visions are not dreams. You don't wake up from a vision and realize it was just a dream. A vision is a compelling picture of the future that is reachable on some level but rarely attainable without significant effort, sacrifice and perhaps a bit of luck along the way.

Napoleon Hill said, "Whatever the mind of man can conceive and believe, it can achieve." If you have not read Napoleon Hill's books, please be advised that your entrepreneurial journey needs to include them. Don't expect references to the Internet or modern business or even the personal computer. Mr. Hill died in 1970, but his insights to success and its impact on our underlying humanness is timeless. He understood people and people may use technology but underneath we remain people bound by our humanness.

Back to the topic at hand – you. If you think your life hasn't turned out the way you planned, it's time for a reality check. What do you really want? Do you have a personal vision? If so, is it specific, actionable, attainable and time-based?

So, how do you create a vision? I include a process that I like below. You may have seen this or something similar to it in INC magazine or other business or success websites. It's a proven technique that's been around for a while and gets republished from time to time.

Steps to create a vision:

First, you're more likely to get what you want out of life if you are intentional about it. To get clear about what you want, start with a set of "Whys."

When you think you want this or that, ask yourself why. Why do you want what you want? Finding the core of what you really want reveals your true desires. Quite often I discover that what I thought I wanted were things someone else wanted for me, and not my actual desires. For example, perhaps a parent wants their child to be a successful doctor. That's what their mom or dad wants for them. Those wishes are noble in that parents obviously want to see their child succeed. But it's not the child's vision.

An even worse scenario embedded is that you might adopt what other people think is best for you and miss out on the opportunity to achieve your own goals. What if the child referenced above loves engineering and dreams of building skyscrapers? They lose that joy. This kind of visioning doesn't stop when we grow up. Each of us can and should have a vision today. And each of us probably has friends and family around us who could interfere or propel the vision just as the parents in the example. With a clear head, it's time to move forward to step two.

Second, create a vision that reflects what actually matters to you. Be careful that you don't focus on money for the sake of money. Money in and of itself CANNOT be your answer. Oh, you may think that money would do it. Is it financial security? A better life for your parents or children? Most people don't get clear about their vision overnight. It requires time for reflection, using both logic and a feeling perspective. Vision comes from your own desires, hopes, dreams and values. When you create a vision that resonates with your purpose and values, it generates energy, passion and commitment; and magical things start to happen.

Here are some guidelines to help you as you reflect on your vision:

The most difficult step in creating a vision is discovering what you truly want. These guidelines can help you discover what matters most to you.

Focus on what really matters to you. Ask, "What do I want to do?" — not "What should I do?"

Ask "Why? Why? Why?" until you have clarity in your heart. Each time you think you have the answer, or maybe just part of the answer, ask yourself "Why do I want that?" Dig down until you find what is fundamentally important to you and you are convinced you are not influenced by anyone else.

Be proactive and create a vision for what you truly desire, not what you want to move away from. Focus on where you want to go, not what you want to leave behind. In regular career, many people jump to a new job because they are running FROM a situation they don't like at their current job. Too many of these people are not running

TO a new and exciting opportunity. They are thinking more about escaping a tough present situation than planning a bright future.

People do virtually the same thing in relationships all the time. How many of your friends have jumped into a short-term, ill-advised "rebound" relationship immediately after breaking off an unhealthy or difficult relationship? It's the same human dynamic at work in relationship as it is in careers.

I assume you get the point about being proactive and thoughtful. Give yourself permission to explore, to dream. Be creative. Be playful. Use your "right brain" – logic can kick-in later.

Spend some relaxed time dreaming and imagining: What will the results look like; what will be accomplished; how will I feel about myself; how will I feel about others. Focus on the end-result, not the process for getting there.

Don't limit yourself by what you may think is possible. "I have a vision to be the have the best bakery in my town" is nice, but "to be the best, most well-known bakery in my state" is more exciting. Notice there is no mention of money? If you start with this vision, the money will be there – it's implied. Having the best bakery means sales and happy customers – the money is there.

On the other hand, if the goal is to make $100,000 per year, then the next question is "OK how do I do that?" So the vision comes first, and the money will follow.

Elon Musk is an amazing and current example of vision. People know him today for Tesla and SpaceX, but his story is deeper and it's a perfect example of having a vision that never stops as life goes on. You could say his vision is to "do innovative things in old industries."

Born and raised in South Africa, Elon Musk purchased his first computer at age 10. He taught himself how to program, and when he was 12 he made his first software sale—of a game he created called Blastar. At age 17, in 1989, he moved to Canada to attend Queen's University, but he left in 1992 to study business and physics at the University of Pennsylvania. He graduated with an undergraduate degree in economics and stayed for a second bachelor's degree in physics.

After leaving Penn, Elon Musk headed to Stanford University in California to pursue a Ph.D. in energy physics. However, his move was timed perfectly with the Internet boom, and he dropped out of Stanford after just two days to become a part of it, launching his first company, Zip2 Corporation.

An online city guide, Zip2 was soon providing content for the new Web sites of both the New York Times and the Chicago Tribune, and in 1999, a division of Compaq Computer Corporation bought Zip2 for $307 million in cash and $34 million in stock options. Was he headed for the beach? Nope! Also in 1999, Musk co-founded X.com, an online financial services/payments company. An X.com acquisition the following year led to the creation of PayPal as it is known today, and in October 2002, PayPal was acquired by eBay for $1.5 billion in stock.

Never one to rest on his laurels, Musk founded his third company, Space Exploration Technologies Corporation, or SpaceX, in 2002 with the intention of building spacecraft for commercial space travel. By 2008, SpaceX was well established, and NASA awarded the company the contract to handle cargo transport for the International Space Station—with plans for astronaut transport in the future—in a move to replace NASA's own space shuttle missions.

The boundless potential of space exploration and the preservation of the future of the human race have become the cornerstones of Musk's abiding interests, and toward these, he has founded the Musk Foundation, which is dedicated to space exploration and the discovery of renewable and clean energy sources.

Along the way, Musk founded Tesla Motors, a company that's now familiar to everyone - dedicated to producing affordable, mass-market electric cars.

On May 22, 2012, Musk and SpaceX made history when the company launched its Falcon 9 rocket into space with an unmanned capsule. The vehicle was sent to the International Space Station with 1,000 pounds of supplies for the astronauts stationed there, marking the first time a private company had sent a spacecraft to the International Space Station. Of the launch, Musk was quoted as saying, "I feel very lucky. ... For us, it's like winning the Super Bowl."

In December 2013, SpaceX notched another milestone when Falcon 9 carried a satellite to geosynchronous transfer orbit, a distance at which the satellite would lock into an orbital path that matched the Earth's rotation. In February 2015, SpaceX launched another Falcon 9 fitted with the Deep Space Climate Observatory (DSCOVR) satellite, aiming to observe the extreme emissions from the sun that affect power grids and communications systems on Earth.

Musk has continued his work in attempting to make his innovative ideas a reality. In August 2013, he released a concept for a new form of transportation called the "Hyperloop," an invention that would foster commuting between major cities while severely cutting travel time. Ideally resistant to weather and powered by renewable energy, the Hyperloop would propel riders in pods through a network of low-pressure tubes at speeds reaching more than 700 mph. Musk noted that the Hyperloop could take from seven to 10 years to be built and ready for use.

Although he introduced the Hyperloop with claims that it would be safer than a plane or train, with an estimated cost of $6 billion—approximately one-tenth of the cost for the rail system planned by the state of California—Musk's concept has drawn skepticism. Nevertheless, the entrepreneur has sought to encourage the development of this idea.

WOW! Now that's vision. Do you think Elon Musk's visions are complete? No way.

What's your vision?

Post-It #2

(Stick it where you will see it every day):

2. VISION:

"I am not

What happened to me,

I am

What I choose to become."

– Carl Jung

3

COMMITMENT

Part Timers, Full Timers and All-Timers

"I'd catch a grenade for you
Throw my hand on a blade for you
I'd jump in front of a train for you
You know I'd do anything for you"
– Bruno Mars, Grenade

We live in a microwave-driven, instant gratification society. We can get anything right now. Amazon Prime ships in one day, iTunes downloads Adele in one minute, a text message gets an answer (from most people) in seconds.

Commitment takes time and achieving even the smallest goal requires you to commit. Throughout your life, you will soon realize that without committing, you can't achieve much of anything. Great goals are not like a bag of microwave popcorn. They take commitment and becoming a success at something meaningful takes commitment. Success without commitment is a lottery ticket.

When we think we see overnight success, what we are really seeing is an illusion. We are blind to the effort it took for the individual to succeed and the passing of time along the way. Multiple popular media outlets have pointed out what songwriter Lisa Loeb said in describing her success, "My overnight success was really 15 years in the making. I'd been writing songs since I was 6 and playing in bands and performing since I was 14."

When I see a young, vibrant Lisa Loeb in her mid-20's on stage, I don't see the passing of time and the commitment that it took to get her onto that stage. If she had not started when she was six (yes, six) then she would not be on that stage today.

When you read Lisa's quote, do you stop to wonder if you could actually match her commitment?

When you reflect on it honestly, everything you have achieved probably started with a specific commitment; whether it's graduating from high school, saving for your first car, your college degree, your job, or even the house you live in.

You must learn how to commit and stay committed in the face of challenges that you know you will encounter as well as those that are unforeseen.

I also see commitment in the form of dedication to vision. I'm fond of pointing out that I've observed three types of people among those who call themselves entrepreneurs. I group these in the following way:

Level 1: Part Timer – 40 hours a week.

Level 2: Full Timer – 60 hours a week

Level 3: All The Timer – 80+ hours a week

At Level 1 are the Part Timers who work as if they work for someone else. The concept of a 40-hour week emerged in the late 1860's. It was actually a labor-based system and the US government enacted legislation while labor unions emerged. Again, this was a labor-based system, not an ownership-based system. Business owners have been working 80+ hour weeks since before the industrial revolution. If you only work 40 hours and are competing against another entrepreneur with a similar idea, you are likely falling behind.

At Level 2 are the Full Timers. These are entrepreneurs who work 20 hours a week longer than their employees. What do they do with this time? They watch their competitors, look for signs in the market, cultivate their own skills and refine their strategies.

At Level 3 are the rare All The Timers. Here you will find the entrepreneurs who essentially double the effort that a Full Timer puts into the above list. All The Timers obsess more deeply than others and are less interested in money (although they have bills to pay like the rest of us) and are more interested in the business they are building.

I love the story about a concert violinist who supposedly said, "If I miss a day of practice, I notice. If I miss two days, my friends notice. If I miss three days, the whole world notices." This violinist was obviously an All The Timer with a vision to be so great that backing off his strict practice regimen would be obvious to the world.

There is also a compelling article that you can read about the work ethic of Elon Musk, Jeff Bezos, and others in the April 2016 issue of INC magazine. It was an incredible dive into the truth of their business tenacity and commitment. Here's a bullet list from that article:

- Apple CEO Tim Cook routinely begins emailing employees at 4:30 in the morning.

- Dallas Mavericks owner Mark Cuban didn't take a

vacation for seven years while starting his first business.

- Amazon CEO Jeff Bezos' high school classmates allegedly gave up when he decided he wanted to be valedictorian – his work ethic was evident even then.

- Venus and Serena Williams were up hitting tennis balls at six a.m. from the time they were seven and eight years old.

- Nissan and Renault CEO Carlos Ghosn flies more than 150,000 miles a year.

- NBA legend Michael Jordan spent his summers taking hundreds of jump shots a day.

- WPP CEO Sir Martin Sorrell is a legendary workaholic whose employees can expect emails at any hour of the night.

- GE CEO Jeffrey Immelt spent 24 years putting in 100-hour weeks.

- Lakers superstar Kobe Bryant completely changed his shooting technique rather than stop playing after breaking a finger.

- Pepsi CEO Indra Nooyi worked the graveyard shift as a receptionist while putting herself through Yale.

- Elon Musk, founder of Tesla simply tells other entrepreneurs they need to work twice as hard as everyone else.

What does that say about All The Timers? It's pretty clear that if you want to lead an industry, you need to understand that commitment has a different meaning than to casually say "commitment."

So many people want to be millionaires, but the majority are NOT looking for the truth about commitment and work ethic. Instead, they are looking for some sort of shortcut that simply does not exist. Truth be told, I believe these people don't want anything to do with being entrepreneurs, they actually want to be lottery winners. What I mean by that is this: they think money is the answer and they will spend time telling you about what they would BUY and DO with that money. That's why they would be broke soon after winning the lottery. Before you start down the lottery path, do a little research on the correlation between suicides and lottery winners. It's not a pretty picture.

I love examples of true committment. Tom exposed me to Formula One racing where true commitment is required to win and years of true commitment are required to ever become a world champion. Along the way I became inspired by the life of three-time Formula One world champion Ayrton Senna. He was a shining example of committment wrapped in passion. He simple didn't know any other way to drive than to fully commit. Senna once said in an now famous interview, "Being a racing driver means you are racing with other peeople and if you no longer go for a [pass] that exists, you are no longer a racing driver because we are competing - - competing to win and the main motivation for all of us is to compete for victory, not to come finish 3rd, 4th, 5th or 6th." He died tragically in 1994 but his legend encourages and insires people even today - including me. Did you notice the name of my daughter?

If you have not ever watched SENNA, the movie about his life, stop reading and go do that NOW. He talks of feeling close to God when he drives. Do you feel closer to God pursuing your passion? It's possible! If you are not inspired by how Senna approached hislife and his career, then it may not be possible to insire you!

My comments about committment invariably lead to a simple question I put to people: what exactly is holding them back? What is the real reason for their lack of commitment?

I found two reasons – thinking small and being afraid

of, or unwilling to do, the hard work.

Those afraid of hard work are usually Level 1 people who think they want to be entrepreneurs but are really only in love with the idea of making or having money, not the idea of making a difference with the business they want to build. Yes, there is a huge difference.

When I think of commitment, I also think of athletes who need to be committed first to training and then to competing and then to winning and finally to winning professional championships or the Olympics.

What better example of commitment is there than Phil Knight of Nike?

Three events shaped Knight's future as the leader of Nike. The first occurred in 1957 when he met Bowerman, his coach on the University of Oregon track team. Bowerman was a former Olympian whose passion for athletes and innovation would eventually inspire Knight to create a business dedicated to those two things. When Knight began his business selling shoes to track athletes, Bowerman became his partner.

The second event occurred when Knight was attending business school at Stanford University. In response to an assignment from Professor Frank Shallenberger, Knight devised a business and marketing plan for importing high-quality running shoes from Japan and selling them in the United States at a high profit margin. In a sense, the vision of Nike was born in that class. The third event occurred in 1963 when Knight traveled to Japan and met with executives from the Onitsuka Company, which distributed Tiger running shoes. Knight talked himself into a distribution contract with the company, and when the executives asked which company he represented, Knight blurted out the first thing to come into his head: Blue Ribbon Sports. The trip initiated Knight's lifelong fascination with Japanese culture and presaged the globalization of Nike.

In 1964 Knight and Bill Bowerman both invested $500 to start Blue Ribbon Sports, which would work together with the Onitsuka Company to develop and distribute running shoes for the North American market. As the company struggled to grow, Knight worked as a certified public accountant and taught at Portland State University. Over the next few years BRS retail stores opened in Santa Monica, California, and Eugene, Oregon, and the company began to assemble employees who would later take on key roles at Nike. In 1969 alone Knight sold $1 million worth of Tiger shoes. By the end of 1971 contract disagreements with Onitsuka prompted Knight and Bowerman to consider starting their own shoe company. Knight paid a former Portland State student to develop the swoosh design, and Jeff Johnson, a Blue Ribbon Sports employee, literally dreamed up the Nike name. The first model of shoe, the Cortez, debuted at the 1972 Olympic trials, and in that first year, Nike had revenues of more than $3 million.

Being an athlete himself, Knight wanted to shape his company around the needs of athletes. He also wanted to create products that the world's greatest athletes would want to use and be associated with. At first, Knight reached out to Olympic track athletes, such as the long-distance runner Steve Prefontaine, who would influence other runners to try the shoes. In 1978 Nike approached the tennis star John McEnroe and signed him to an endorsement deal. This choice of spokesperson reflected Knight's vision that the great athlete was the ultimate free spirit. By 1980, Nike had captured one-half of the athletic shoe market and carried out its initial public offering on the New York Stock Exchange. The escalating wealth of the company allowed Nike to sign additional top-flight athletes to endorsement contracts, including highly lucrative relationships with Michael Jordan and Tiger Woods.

Knight was vigilant to keep Nike at the top of the industry. In the late 1980s, when Reebok briefly supplanted Nike as the most profitable athletic shoe company, Knight streamlined the Nike campus in Beaverton, Oregon, and gave it a corporate atmosphere while maintaining the image of a company run by casually rebellious athletes. In the 1990s, despite criticism, Knight involved the company in environmental and community service activities. At the same time Nike branched out into hockey, golf, and soccer apparel, opened huge Niketown stores in shopping malls, and continued its dominance in the area of track-and-field apparel. As the result of this aggressive expansion, Nike had more than $10 billion in yearly sales before 1999.

Knight was said to be not fond of advertising. Yet slogans such as "Just do it" and images such as that of Michael Jordan soaring through the air cemented Nike's place in the industry. Nike advertisements portrayed great athletes as objects worthy of worship but also implied that everyone has greatness within themselves.

Everyone I know has been motivated some way by Nike and "Just do it." It's a vision statement and call to execute bundles into three simple words.

Stay Committed! How? Just Do It!

Post-It #3

(Stick it where you will see it every day)

3. COMMITMENT:

"Stay committed to your Decisions, but stay flexible in your approach."

– Anthony "Tony" Robbins

4

RESILIENCY

How to Keep Fighting

"I'm gonna change you like a remix
Then I'll raise you like a phoenix."
– Phoenix, Fall Out Boy

If there is one guarantee in life, it is that there will be heartbreak and then more heartbreak. People will let you down, and it will hurt more when it is people you love and trust such as friends and relatives. People will die. The economy will turn. A business you create or one you work for will rise and fall and maybe rise again – or not. Faced by all of those challenges, if you want to stay in the game and have a chance at true success, you must persevere and perseverance is not perseverance without resiliency.

Resiliency is defined as "a quality in objects that allows them to recover their shape." If you bend a tree branch, and it flexes right back — that's resiliency. In people, resiliency is more about bending the invisible spirit within each of us – but not breaking it. In people like you, it's the ability to "stay intact" emotionally and not to break in the face of challenges or obstacles. Thus, resiliency is a kind of personal strength, and it's one that you can learn from personal experience and encouragement from others.

Developing personal resiliency requires that you not break emotionally and you simultaneously do something positive with the pain of setbacks. Along the way, you cannot allow setbacks to become excuses. This is where a parent, teacher, friend or mentor can be a critical partner in your growth and development. These people know you better than anyone else and can be trusted 24X7.

One way you can break is to take the easy way out and use challenges or setbacks as an excuse NOT to try. I talked about that in Chapter 1 - Truth. How many people do you know who have quit along the way toward a goal they had set for themselves? Is one of them looking at you in the mirror? The opposite of resiliency is breaking – commonly known as quitting. You can have a wonderful vision, be committed to it early on in your journey, but a lack of resiliency can bring it crashing down around you.

Basketball legend Michael Jordan said, "I can accept

failure, everyone fails at something. But I can't accept not trying." If you read between the lines of Michael Jordan's quote you can sense the encouragement to continue pushing in the face of failure – that's resiliency.

Many books and articles have been written about how to build resiliency. With those and our own experience in mind, here is our blueprint:

5 Steps to Building Resiliency

1. Maintain a positive attitude

This may seem obvious, but maintaining a positive attitude is critical to building resilience. Remember, that you're in control how you respond, whether you think the glass is half-empty or half-full.

2. Establish a support network

I don't know of anyone who can truly "go it alone," as the saying goes. You would do well to build a list of three to five close relationships with friends and mentors who can lift your spirits, encourage your performance and challenge your attitude during the tough times. Finding a mentor is an art of its own and much is written about it.

3. Take care of you

I believe in fitness in the form of regular exercise and

limited caffeine and sugar consumption. While I am not a licensed nutritionist, I know what I have seen and personally experienced. Regular physical activity has been linked to reduced stress, improved mental sharpness and, not surprisingly, self-esteem. Setting aside time for exercise may seem unimportant when you are short on time and another soda or cup of coffee may perk you up for a moment – but I think the benefits are clear.

4. Play to your strengths

Recognize, grow and live in what you do best. If you have strong aptitudes here or there or you want to develop them, ask your support network to keep you accountable to do so. Doing what you're good at (or simply what you enjoy doing) will also invariably lead to 'wins' along the way which builds your confidence.

5. Be the doctor

This is one of my favorites. Think of yourself as a doctor in an emergency room. When an ER doctor encounters a child with a bee sting, it's a simple day at the office. On the other hand, when paramedics rush in with an unconscious car accident victim, it's not a simple day at the office. The problems are complex, and there is no time to make excuses while the family of the victim is praying in the waiting room. There is only time to think one thought: "what am I seeing RIGHT NOW and what can I do about it RIGHT NOW with the team and medical tools I have with me RIGHT NOW." If you want to build reflexes that are resilient and immune to excuses, a simple drill is to start each day by closing your eyes and meditating on that last sentence. You are training your brain to be resilient in the face of the challenges you will inevitably face.

I see resiliency in champion athletes, and I applaud it. Do you ever look at yourself and say – I am an individual person just like that athlete? Probably not. Well, the truth is, yes you are! These public figures are flesh and blood just like you. Although they perform in front of TV cameras and crowds of people, they are also just like you when it comes to vision, commitment, and resiliency. Unlike you, I can watch them build their own resiliency over the course of their careers.

Al Unser Jr is a great example. He is a champion racing driver and won the Indianapolis 500 twice. But did you know what he encountered on the journey? It took him 10 years and 10 attempts to win it for the first time in 1992, and he won it again only two years later in 1994. Along the way, he wondered if he would ever win it but he never stopped trying. He never quit.

For Al Unser Jr., winning the Indy-500 was a lifelong dream. His father won it four times, and his uncle won it three times. He came from a family of champions, but he never took that for granted because their achievements did not mean he would automatically be a champion. Al knew that while his dad may have helped open some doors for him, HE had to drive the car – no one could do it for him, and if he didn't prove to be a winner, he'd have to find another line of work.

Unlike an individual who got a job in the family business and could hide their incompetence or poor performance behind closed doors, in auto racing your report card is printed on the sports page every weekend. In other words, Al Unser Jr. had no place to hide if he couldn't make the cut.

Al encountered adversity and setbacks along the way to achieving his dream. For example, in 1989, he was a mere one lap away from winning the Indy-500 when he was bumped by another driver and crashed. Fortunately, he was not hurt physically, but it certainly hurt mentally to be less than 60 seconds away from achieving a lifelong dream only to have it snatched away in such cruel fashion.

But Al was resilient and stayed focused on his vision. A year later he again missed winning the Indy-500, but he won the season championship in dominating fashion, including a stretch where he won four races in a row.

In 1992, Al was in a car that was not as fast as two other cars that were heavy favorites and expected to win the Indy 500 by a wide margin. Despite this challenge, Al approached the race with tenacity. He drove smart and made it up to 2nd place when, only 10 laps from the end, the leader's car broke down. Al and another driver then fought a close battle neck and neck, and he won the Indy-500 in the most thrilling finish in history. The journey took 10 years of resiliency and, importantly, not ever giving up – especially on the one improbable day that he would realize his dream.

Two years later in 1994 Al had the privilege of driving the fastest car and made the most of the opportunity. He won the Indy-500 again, joining an elite group of racing drivers, including his father and uncle, who won the race more than once. He also won the season championship again that year, placing himself among the greats in auto racing history.

It took Al Unser Jr. 10 years to achieve his dream, but he remained committed to his vision and was resilient along the way. What if he had quit? Many drivers with similar dreams did quit. Not Al Unser Jr.

Composer Franz Liszt said, "Real men are sadly lacking in this world, for when they are put to the test they prove worthless." Liszt is talking about breaking versus being resilient.

You may not race in the Indy-500 in front of hundreds of thousands of people and millions more watching on TV, but that does not matter. You can apply the same commitment and resiliency to your own journey.

Your victories and setbacks along the way will have different names, but the human spirit inside you is the same as Al Unser Jr. or any other business leader, celebrity or athlete.

Post-It #4

(Stick it where you will see it every day)

4. RESILIENCY:

I am certain

I have the inner strength

to bounce back from

any setback or challenge.

5

VALIDATION

Be Patient – It Will Come

"Say oh, got this feeling that you can't fight
Like this city is on fire tonight
This could really be a good life
A good, good life"
– Good Life OneRepublic

One of the most satisfying feelings in the world is that of winning." In addition to winning in the traditional sense where an opponent is defeated, it can take a couple other more subtle forms; being correct, achieving a milestone, etc.

Let's review the first several chapters. First, you have decided to embrace the truth. Then, you have set a vision that is followed by making the decision to commit to stay with it and remain resilient in the face of obstacles. If you have done all of that, then you will be working hard and awaiting some point of validation.

Validation is where your decision is confirmed by the first measures of success. Perhaps it's the first big sale after you become a life insurance agent. Maybe it's the first customer for your new online business. Whatever form it takes, you eagerly seek, and pray for, some point of validation. The journey may be long and that's why the previous chapter focused on resiliency!

The point of validation is where entrepreneurs find what they call traction. There's a great book called, "Traction: How Any Startup Can Achieve Explosive Customer Growth" by Gabriel Weinberg and Justin Mares. In that book, Gabriel and Justin discuss a series of issues related to traction. Doing several small things simultaneously to stimulate marketing and sales – but in the same direction and with a consistent strategy to see what and when you can get the business to move.

This book introduces entrepreneurs to the "Bullseye Framework," a five-step process successful companies use to get traction. This framework helps founders find the marketing channel that will be key to unlocking the next stage of growth.

The concept is similar to "Tipping Point" a book by Malcolm Gladwell. The tipping point is that magic moment when an idea, trend, or social behavior crosses a threshold, tips, and spreads like wildfire. Just as a single sick person can start an epidemic of the flu, so too can a small but precisely targeted push cause a fashion trend, or drive the popularity of a new product.

Both books talk a lot about the "other side" – when victory can now be seen. The underlying theme is that commitment and resiliency lead to traction and get you over the tipping point. Some entrepreneurs call this the "at last!" moment. Of course, great entrepreneurs are all-the-timers and those see validation as the starting gun in the race for taking a piece of the new market!

You probably have noticed that I have referenced a number of books. There's a very good reason for that: Successful entrepreneurs are readers and take every opportunity to learn from others who have walked the entrepreneurial path. There is a list of the top 100 books for entrepreneurs listed at www.patrickbatdavid.com.

Speaking of books, when I think of validation, I think about Jeff Bezos – who turned Amazon into the biggest bookstore in the world!

When you read his story, you see validation over and over again. Is he just lucky? NO! He always had a vision, he never gave up and he always thought about even bigger things after he experienced each victory.

I've read short and long versions of Jeff Bezos biography in magazines and on the Internet. I think the best compilation comes from a 1999 Wired magazine article that was blended with more up to date information by a couple reporters at Business Insider. The irony is that Bezos has an investment in Business Insider so they better get his story straight! I've taken facts and such from that article with my assumption being that a biography about how you grew up doesn't change much!

Jeff was born in 1964 to a teenage mom - 19-year-old year old Jackie Bezos and 20-year-old Mike Bezos. Jeff found out that Mike was not his biological father when he was 10 years old. He has absolutely no hang-ups about it.

Jeff explained to Wired Magazine in 1999, "The reality, as far as I'm concerned, is that my Dad is my natural father. The only time I ever think about it, genuinely, is when a doctor asks me to fill out a form,"

Jeff spent summers during childhood summers at his grandparents' home in Texas. He castrated cattle and performed a litany of other farm chores. Jeff's grandfather was significant role model in these early years. His name was Lawrence Preston "Pop" Gise and he worked in the space industry and supervised over 25,000 employees.

As a kid, Jeff never talked about being a spaceman but he did say things about being a space entrepreneur. In school, Jeff told teachers "the future of mankind is not on this planet." Today, Jeff owns a space exploration company called Blue Origin. I imagine the influence of his grandfather played a role in the vision for Blue Origin.

When Jeff was 12, he was featured in a book called "Turning on Bright Minds: A Parent Looks at Gifted Education in Texas." The book described Bezos as "friendly but serious" and "not particularly gifted in leadership." They got that only half right!

Barely above the weight limit, Jeff joined a youth pee wee football team. Jackie Bezos would later comment, "I thought he was going to get creamed out there," He became team captain because he was the only one of the players who could remember all of the plays.

As a teenager, Jeff worked for a summer at a McDonald's. He absolutely hated it. So the next summer, Jeff and his girlfriend founded an education camp for younger kids.

They called their camp "The DREAM Institute," They charged $600 per child and got six signups. The camp's required reading gives a look into Jeff Bezo's right and left-brain mind. In the Wired article he listed: The Once and Future King, Stranger in a Strange Land, The Lord of the Rings, Dune, Watership Down, Black Beauty, Gulliver's Travels, Treasure Island, and David Copperfield, along with the plays Our Town and The Matchmaker.

Jeff attended Princeton and after college, he became employee number 11 at a startup called Fitel. The job was a grind as he was flying between New York and London every week. "This is not the right way to organize a startup company," Jeff mused in an interview.

Next came a job with Bankers Trust. Jeff almost quit that job to found a news-by-fax service startup with Halsey Minor, who would later found CNET. Instead, Jeff quit Bankers Trust to work for D.E. Shaw's hedge fund. He cruised to a SVP title in four years.

During this period, Jeff established a systematic process – the "women flow" – to help him with his next big life milestone: finding a wife. The same way Venture Capitalists and Wall Street bankers establish future "Deal

Flows,: Bezos created a "women flow."

Bezos said he wanted a woman who could "get me out of a Third World Prison." He told Wired, "What I really wanted was someone resourceful. But nobody knows what you mean when you say, 'I'm looking for a resourceful woman.' If I tell somebody I'm looking for a woman who can get me out of a Third World prison, they start thinking Ross Perot - Ah-ha-ha-ha-ha-ha! - they have something they can hang their hat on! Life's too short to hang out with people who aren't resourceful."

He eventually married an office-mate named Mackenzie. She's now a novelist and mother to their four children.

Despite DE Shaw's protests, Bezos quit to start Amazon. On a long walk in Central Park, Shaw tried to talk Jeff out of quitting, but Jeff couldn't get over the fact that the Internet was growing 2,400% per year.

Bezos simply decided he'd rather try and fail at a startup than never try at all. In Seattle, Jeff and his first employee, Shel Kaphan, built Amazon.com in a garage with a potbellied stove.

They built the site around the huge digital catalogs book distributors started using in the 1980s and in an ultimate irony, Jeff held most of his meetings at the neighborhood Barnes & Noble. In fact, Amazon's first freight contracts were negotiated at a Barnes & Noble in Seattle. Could anyone have envisioned at that time that he would later nearly crush Barnes & Noble?

Bezos and Kaphan were off and running set up a bell to ring every time Amazon.com made a sale. They turned it off after a couple weeks because it wouldn't stop. The bell is a fitting metaphor for ongoing validation that has greeted Jeff Bezos over and over again.

Barely two years later Amazon's initial public offering was made in 1997. It was a success, but not without skeptics. Some analysts called the company "Amazon-dot-bomb."

But Amazon has survived and thrived for two reasons: (1) Users kept coming to the site in bigger numbers, and (2) Jeff never promised shareholders anything but a long-term vision. In 2009, Amazon turned 14 and its stock was up 5000% since its IPO.

Amazon.com started with a vision to deliver a great experience to customers shopping for books. Was Bezos just lucky? Nope. Under Bezos direction Amazon poured time and energy into other segments and they have also done incredibly well:

Selling books led to selling eBooks which led to the Kindle. Along the way Kindle direct publishing enables anyone to be an eBook author.

Selling books also led to selling other media such as DVDs which led to Amazon Video, a pay per view video service that is now found pre-loaded on many digital TVS.

Being a massive online store led Bezos to use the technology that powered Amazon.com to enable other stores and feature their inventory on Amazon.com Today there are thousands and thousands of affiliate merchants.

What's Bezos next target? As this book was published (by Amazon), he announced the launch of a competitor to YouTube. There's ambitious and then there's *ambitious*. I believe attacking YouTube is the latter.

Jeff Bezos did not get lucky. He had a vision that was a success and once it was validated he couldn't help himself and developed other visions which also became successful.

Will you be another Jeff Bezos? The odds are long but only those who dare to turn a dream into a plan have a chance to find out.

Post-It #5

(Stick it where you will see it every day)

5. VALIDATION:

At first they will ask

WHY I did it.

Later they will ask

HOW I did it.

6

DRIFT OR DRIVE

Are You All-In?

"Drifting through the wind only to start again."

– Firework by Katie Perry

I have set the table for you in the first five chapters. It's now up to you whether you drift through life or drive forward with a plan. The life of an entrepreneur has been outlined for you:

1. Entrepreneurs embrace TRUTH

They accept their reality and move forward.

2. Entrepreneurs have specific VISION

They look forward to something specific.

3. Entrepreneurs have COMMITMENT

They stay with their vision.

4. Entrepreneurs have RESILIENCY

They bounce-back and recover from setbacks.

5. Entrepreneurs watch for VALIDATION

They believe confirmation is coming.

You now have a choice – to drift through life as you may have been doing or to drive through life with an intentional framework. Remember my comments at the beginning of this book? Which person will you be?

The toughest part of any journey is actually not not planning – it's taking the first step to be resolved to change your mindset, make a plan and THEN take the first step.

Have you ever gone skydiving? Planning isn't tough. Step one is to choose a local school, give them a couple hundred dollars and sit in a class to learn about skydiving. None of that is tough. Step 2 is getting on a plane with 15 other people, which also isn't tough. Stepping out of the plane BY YOURSELF is tough.

There are other examples from childhood as well. Remember the first time you jumped off a diving board as a child? That diving board looked a mile high!

In the US we all can choose to drift or drive. If we choose to drive, that requires taking the all-important first step. We have the luxury of freedom in this country and frankly too many of us take it for granted. Before you interrupt me in your mind, I am not talking about Gen X, Millennials and Gen Y – I am talking to *everybody*.

There are great stories from other countries and while I hope to be one of them, one of my favorite stories is that of András Gróf. He is better known as Andy Grove, the management guru that drove Intel, the company that probably made the chip in the computer you used today or in the servers that power the Internet you accessed from your smartphone.

Andy was born in Budapest, Hungary, in 1936. When he was only eight, the Germans invaded Hungary and the Nazis sent 500,000 Jews to concentration camps. Grove recounts assuming a false identity along with his mother, and somehow being hidden away by friends until the occupation ended. His childhood consisted of experiencing war, insecurity, fear and one of the most horrific events in human history in which his grandmother, his Father's mother, was killed at Auschwitz, the notorious concentration camp.

In 1956, Grove was 20 and most people his age were thinking about college or what to do in life. In Budapest Hungary, Grove had no such choice. The Hungarian Revolution started and he was forced to escape to Austria and then came to America thanks in part to assistance from a humanitarian organization.

So, what did Andy Grove do in the first seven years he was in America? He got an education. After obtaining a bachelor's degree in New York, Grove went to California, where he earned a PhD in 1963 from the University of California at Berkeley.

Upon his graduation in 1963, he went to work for Fairchild Semiconductor, a small company which had recently been created by a few of the more forward-thinking engineers on the West Coast. It was there he met Bob Noyce and Gordon Moore. Frustrated by Fairchild's lack of vision, Noyce and Moore secured the backing of a prominent venture capitalist and launched Intel. From there the recruitment of Andy Grove was not difficult.

Richard Tedlow wrote a biography on Grove and described Grove's early days at Intel: Andy Grove made the difficult transition from technologist to technologist/manager because he had no choice. When Intel was founded in July of 1968, he was employee number three. Employees number one and two were the founders; Bob Noyce and Gordon Moore. They were older than Andy and did not enjoy the management side of business. That responsibility fell to Andy.

So if Intel was going to be driven, Andy Grove, employee number three, had to do it. Grove admitted he knew very little about managing a business and once said, "I was scared to death. It was terrifying. I literally had nightmares. I was supposed to be director of engineering, but there were so few of us that they made me director of operations."

From there Grove drove hard and never allowed Intel to drift. His tenacious work ethic and demanding management style, while often criticized, brought massive profits for Intel. In 1979, he became president of the company. Four years later, he published *High Output Management*, which was subsequently translated into 11 languages.

Andy Grove became known for being driven and driving Intel with systems and processes that were simple and, most importantly, could be replicated and measured. He also wrote for the Wall Street Journal on the topic of management and Intel's drove profits throughout the 1980's. In 1987 he became CEO.

In 1994, seven years after Grove became CEO, Intel held 90% of the semiconductor market and at one point was the most valuable company in America. Two years later he published *Only the Paranoid Survive,* which would become a timeless management classic.

When I think of Andy Grove, I don't think of a visionary like Steve Jobs, a charismatic risk taker like Richard Branson or a perpetual innovator like Jeff Bezos. No, Andy Grove is from the operational side of the house and he proved yet again that success can come from different angles as long as you are resolved to DRIVE not DRIFT.

Which one are you?

Post-It #6
(Stick it where you will see it every day)

6. ALL-IN:

I Choose to DRIVE

Not DRIFT!

APPENDIX I

THE COMPLETE LIST

1. *TRUTH:*
   I accept the truth of today's reality
   and personally commit to change it.

2. ***VISION:***
   "I am not what happened to me, I am what I choose to become." – Carl Jung

3. ***COMMITMENT:***
   "I will stay committed to my vision, but I will remain flexible in my approach." – Tony Robbins

4. ***RESILIENCY:***
   I am certain I have the inner strength to bounce back from any set-back or challenge that I encounter.

5. ***VALIDATION:***
   At First They Will Ask WHY
   I did it, later they will ask HOW I did it.

6. ***DRIFT OR DRIVE:***
   ALL-In: I choose to Drive not Drift!

ABOUT THE AUTHORS

Patrick Bet-David

Patrick's amazing story starts with his family immigrating to America when he was 10-years old. His parents fled Iran as refugees during the Iranian revolution and were eventually granted U.S. citizenship.

After high school Patrick joined the U.S. military and served in the 101st Airborne before starting a business career in the financial services industry. After a tenure with a couple traditional companies, he was inspired to launch PHP Agency Inc., an insurance sales, marketing and distribution company – and did so before he turned 30. PHP is now one of the fastest growing companies in the financial marketplace.

Patrick is passionate about shaping the next generation of leaders by teaching thought provoking perspectives on entrepreneurship and disrupting the traditional approach to a career. Patrick's popularity surged and created a buzz in the hearts of entrepreneurs all over the world when The Life of an Entrepreneur in 90 Seconds, a video he created, accumulated over 27 million views online. This and scores of other videos comprise his library of edifying, educational and inspirational content about entrepreneurship – all available at Valuetainment, a media brand he conceived and founded.

Valuetainment exists to teach about the fundamentals of entrepreneurship and personal development while inspiring people to break from limiting beliefs or other constraints and achieve their dreams. It has been referred to as "the voice for entrepreneurs."

Patrick speaks on a range of business, leadership and entrepreneurial topics including how and why to become an entrepreneur and the importance of learning how to fully process issues. He is particularly passionate about the need for every individual to pursue their desires, once stating, "Most of the greatest world changers and heroes of all time are at the graveyard undiscovered because they never sold out to their dreams and desires."

Patrick has also hosted a series of one-on-one interviews with some of the world's most interesting people, including NBA Hall of Famer James Worthy, Author Robert Greene, Billionaire and Entrepreneur Mark Cuban, Indy-500 Winner Al Unser Jr., Apple co-founder, Steve Wozniak, author and entrepreneur Robert Kiyosaki, and many others.

From a humble beginning as a young immigrant escaping war-torn Iran with his parents, to founding his own company, Patrick has gained a first-hand understanding of what rags-to-riches means and how it is fueled by freedom and opportunity – the core tenants of the American Dream.

Patrick resides in Dallas TX with his wife and three children. You can visit Patrick and his books and library of Valuetainment content at:

www.patrickbetdavid.com

Thomas N. Ellsworth

Tom is an experienced CEO, C-Level mentor & author with a passion for professional development that drives his credo; "Leave People Better Than You Found Them."

A veteran entrepreneur, Ellsworth's first start-up was a surfboard repair business that took over the garage at his parent's house. The thriving business closed when his parents essentially evicted him and sent him to college.

Following college he began a career that has enabled him to be part of Venture-backed and mid-stage companies that have generated transactions / exits totaling over $1B.

Currently Ellsworth is President and COO of PHP Agency Inc. where he works with Patrick Bet-David on a crusade to change the life insurance industry.

Previously Ellsworth was CEO and Chairman of Premier Digital Publishing, "PHP," a developer of eBook distribution technology and eBook publisher until acquisition of the publishing division by a large New York publisher in May of 2013.

Before PDP, Ellsworth was CEO of GoTV Networks, a provider of rich media applications. GoTV was the go-to partner for brands and media owners including the NFL and NASCAR. Ellsworth led the company through a complete financial and strategic turnaround followed by successful exit by acquisition in 2011.

Prior to GoTV, Ellsworth served as Executive Vice President, Marketing and Corporate Development at JAMDAT Mobile. Inc. (NASDAQ: JMDT), the largest wireless games publisher in the world. He was a core member of senior management team that drove the start-up to its highly successful IPO (later acquired by Electronic Arts).

In advance of JAMDAT he was Vice President of the eCompanies Wireless Startup Incubator, a Corporate Venture Capital project for Sprint. He managed the fund that identified and invested in start-up companies including JAMDAT, Boingo and Helio.

He received his Bachelor of Science degree in Business Administration; Marketing from California State University, Northridge and an MBA from Pepperdine University.

Today, Tom calls Dallas, Texas home along with his wife and two children. You can visit Tom and his library of business books and blogs at:

www.tomellsworth.com

SPEAKING REQUESTS

To inquire about speaking requests for the author, please send an email with information about the engagement including date, location, size of audience and any other details to: marketing@patrickbetdavid.com

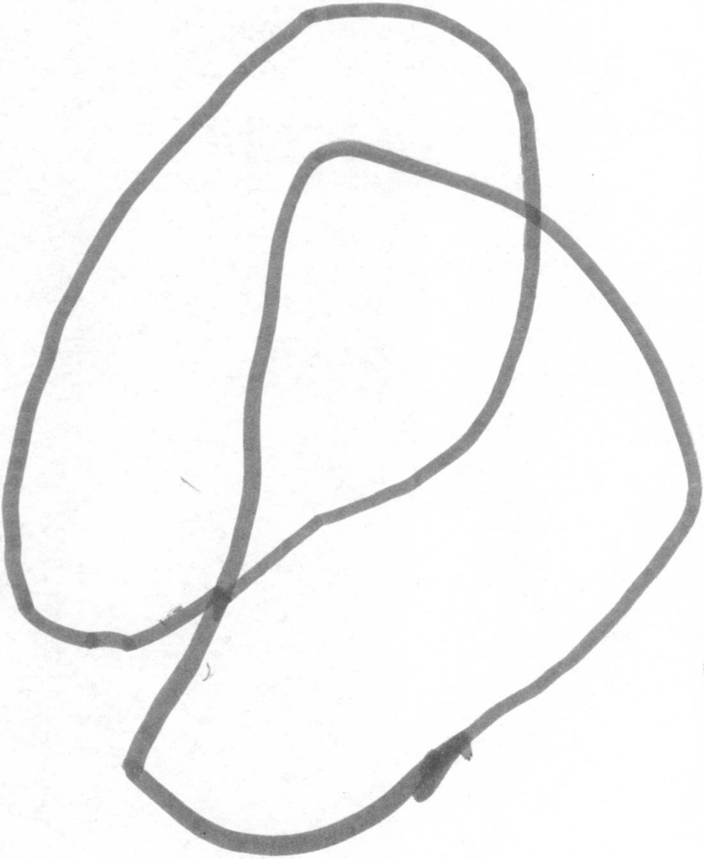

Made in the USA
Lexington, KY
14 June 2016